My family enjoys
Seven miles is our daily minimum. We also like art, history, and food. When researching our trip to Scandinavia about a year ago I consulted multiple travel guides and websites. I also did a lot of googling.

It was clear we had to visit the capitals, but I also wanted to cruise along a Norwegian fjord. My son just finished studying the Viking Age at school and was excited to do all things "Viking." I am a big fan of petroglyphs so when I stumbled across a reference about Bronze Age rock art in Norway I made sure we see it.

In the end I came up with an 11-day itinerary to see Norway, Sweden, and Finland. After making the trip I decided to publish the guide so it can help travelers organize their journey to Scandinavia and the Nordic countries.

When using this guide keep in mind that:

- All hotels, restaurants, and transportation routes are based on firsthand experiences by me and my family.
- Travel time is from late June to early August.
- A traveler has an iPhone or another smart phone with the ability to get walking and driving directions overseas.

Helpful Country Facts

Norway:	Sweden:
Population: 5,597,924 (2023 est.)	*Population:* 10,536,338 (2023 est.)
Capital: Oslo	*Capital:* Stockholm
Language: Norwegian	*Language:* Swedish
Currency: Norwegian krone (NOK) $1=11.15NOK (Sep 18, 2023)	*Currency:* Swedish krona (SEK) $1=11.15SEK (Sep 18, 2023)
GDP per capita (2017 US$) $65,700 (2021 est.)	*GDP per capita* (2017 US$) $53,600 (2021 est.)
Hello = Hallo/hei	Hello = Hej
Thank you = Takk	Thank you = Tack
Finland:	USA:
Population: 5,614,571 (2023 est.)	*Population:* 339,665,118 (2023 est.)
Capital: Helsinki	*Capital:* Washington DC
Language: Finnish	*Language:* English
Currency: Euro (EUR) $1=0.94 EUR (Sep 18, 2023)	*GDP per capita* (2017 US$) $63,700 (2021 est.)
GDP per capita (2017 US$) $48,800 (2021 est.)	
Hello = Hei	
Thank you = Kiitos	

Notes: Currency data is from forbes.com and country data is from CIA world factbook. Retrieved on Sep 18, 2023.

Day 0: Fly into Oslo and check into hotel

Take a taxi or bus from Oslo Airport to the hotel.

Hotel: Radisson Blu Scandinavia Hotel is a typical business hotel that is located in the city center close to the Royal Palace. https://www.radissonhotels.com/en-us/hotels/radisson-blu-oslo-scandinavia

Day 1: Explore Oslo

View of the Royal Palace in the distance from Karl Johans gate in Oslo, Norway

Morning: Take a tour of the **Royal Palace**, which is just a short walk from the hotel. The palace is open to the public in the summer months and guided tours are provided in Norwegian and English. We took a tour in Norwegian as there was no availability in English that day. We were given a paper copy of a tour information in English. For more information and to book tickets go to https://www.royalcourt.no/

Lunch: Have lunch at **Din Deli**. It is a nice small place that is close to the Royal Palace. https://www.dindeli.no/

Afternoon: Visit **Historical Museum** to see relics from the Viking Age. Ideally, you would want to go to the Viking Ship Museum, however, it is closed for renovations until 2026/27 and your best bet for Viking Age artifacts in Oslo is the Historical Museum.
https://www.historiskmuseum.no/english/

Next, walk over to the **Oslo City Hall** and enjoy looking at the murals and other art depicting Norwegian folklore and working life. https://www.oslo.kommune.no/oslo-city-hall/#gref

One of the best-preserved Viking helmets at the Historical Museum in Oslo, Norway

Continue exploring Oslo by walking along **Karl Johans gate**, the main street that stretches from the Royal Palace to the Oslo Central Station. You can stop at the **Oslo Cathedral** and/or take a photo with the Tiger Statue. Pop into **Paradis Gelateria** for a sweet treat and coffee https://www.iskrembar.no/

Dinner: Have a dinner at **Vaaghals restaurant** that serves contemporary Norwegian cuisine. You can book a table on their website. https://www.vaaghals.com/pageen

Evening: After dinner walk to the **Oslo Opera House** and enjoy the sunset.

Day 2: Train to Flam

Morning/Afternoon: Have breakfast at the hotel, pack up and check out. Either walk or take a taxi to Oslo Central Station to catch the train to Flam. We took a 12 o'clock train.

View from a train window at Myrdal, Norway

Train to Flam Booking Details: You will take two trains to get to Flam.

- **Train 1:** from Oslo Central Station (Oslo S) to Myrdal Station (stasjon). This train continues all the way to Bergen.
- **Train 2:** from Myrdal Station (stasjon) to Flam Station (stasjon).

Book your tickets on https://www.vy.no/en You can book about two months in advance. I booked a separate compartment for our family. You can get a decent lunch and snacks on board and don't snooze too much as the scenery is spectacular, especially the last hour from Oslo to Myrdal. Even though it may seem too overwhelming to take two trains in a foreign country, in reality it is not that hard. Most people speak English and can point you in the right direction. Just ask.

Don't forget to book the return trip. You will take the same trains just in reverse.

Hotels in Flam: We stayed two nights in Flam, so we had one full day to enjoy the longest Norwegian fjord, the Sognefjord. There are two main hotels in town, and we ended up spending one night in each as there was no availability for a room for the four of us for two consecutive nights.

1. **Fretheim Hotel**, an older hotel. You can book your stay through
   https://www.norwaysbest.com/fretheim-hotel/

2. **Flamsbrygga Hotel**, a newer hotel and much better than Fretheim in my opinion.
   https://www.flamsbrygga.com/hotel

Dinner: Have dinner at the hotel. Since we stayed our first night at the Fretheim hotel we had their buffet style dinner.

Evening: After dinner walk to the Flam Church and enjoy the feel of being in a fjord village. Outside the hotel turn left and follow the main road Nedre Freithem which will merge with and become Flamsdalsvegen. The road is shared by cars, bikes, and pedestrians so pay attention. Walk to the church. Retrace your steps to get back.

Flam Church in Flam, Norway

Day 3: Fjord Tour to Gudvangen, the Viking Village

Morning: Take a boat tour from Flam to Gudvangen. Book tickets through Norway's Best website https://www.norwaysbest.com/ The tour is called "Fjord Cruise Nærøyfjord."

We took a 9:30 am boat from Flam and it took us about 2 hours to arrive in Gudvangen. The scenery is amazing: countless waterwalls, picturesque villages along the shores, and morning mist. If you are too cold, there are plenty of seats inside and there is a café as well to get a warm drink and a snack.

Leaving Flam on a boat in Flam, Norway

The main attraction in Gudvangen is the **Viking Village**, where a community of people live like Vikings did many centuries ago. Some only live in the summer whereas a few stay year-round. For more information visit their website
https://www.uk.vikingvalley.no/

Lunch: Have lunch at the **Viking Village café**. We opted for some traditional dishes with potatoes and pork.

Afternoon: Take a tour of the Viking Village to learn about Viking history and the village. There are plenty of activities for kids to partake in such as archery, axe throwing, and playing the drums.

We were interested in a hike but there was no official trail to go on to. After asking several people who work at the local shops, we decided to take a walk along the fjord towards Bakka. If you decide to do it just ask someone. You will start at the dock on a road, then take a trail along the shore, which later will merge back with the road.

While waiting for our return boat we had coffee and sweets at the **Gudvangen Coffee Shop and Bakery** located at the dock. One can take a bus back from Gudvangen to Flam. But I wanted to maximize our time in the fjords and so we took the boat back.

Viking Village in Gudvangen, Norway

Dinner: We had dinner at a restaurant at **Flamsbrygga Hotel**. There is also **Aegir Brewery** but it was too busy at the time we were ready to eat. I highly recommend making reservations for dinner in Flam.

Day 4: Return to Oslo, visit Munch Museum and Vigeland Park

Morning/Early Afternoon: Take a train from Flam to Myrdal and then from Myrdal to Oslo. We left Flam's station around 8:30 am and arrived in Oslo around 3 o'clock in the afternoon (or 15:00). Have lunch on the train.

Late Afternoon: Once in Oslo walk over to the **Munch Museum** https://www.munchmuseet.no/en/ You can store your luggage in lockers. Munch (pronounced as Moonk) is famous for his Scream paintings. The museum has three of them and they have only one on display per hour while the other two stay in the darkness. Since we arrived at the museum after 3:30 pm (or 15:30) we were able to see two versions of the Scream.

After the museum we went back to the same **Radisson Blu Scandinavia Hotel**.

Dinner: We had dinner at **Lofotstua restaurant**. This restaurant is advertised in many guides. The restaurant owner, who is also the chef, orders only a small quantity of seafood daily and, therefore, sells out very quickly. Seafood is fresh and is served with French style sauces, potatoes, and a green salad. I made reservations by email. Their website is https://lofotstua-as.business.site/

Evening: The restaurant is close to another famous sightseeing spot, **Vigeland Park**. Take a stroll in the park to see over 200 sculptures by Gustav Vigeland, nudity on full display. Make sure to take a selfie with the famous angry boy.
For more information see
https://vigeland.museum.no/en/vigelandpark

The Angry Boy in Vigeland Park in Oslo, Norway

Day 5: Bronze Age Rock Art in Norway and drive to Stockholm

Morning: Rent a car from Hertz located near the Radisson Blu Scandinavia Hotel and drive to see the Bronze Age petroglyphs at Gullskar Rock Carving Field.

Getting to Gullskar Rock Carving Field: Drive towards Fredrikstad from Oslo. It takes about an hour to get there. I could not get precise GPS coordinates to this site on Apple maps but I set the location for Begby and then followed the road signs to the historical attraction, Gullskår helleristningsfelt (Gullskar Rock Carving Field). It is on Begbyveien road, the closest intersection is Begbyveien and Haldenveien.

The Begby Man at Gullskar Rock Carving Field in Norway

Near the small parking lot there is a display board that provides a brief overview of the rock carvings. The rock carvings at Begby are painted in red so you can't miss them. There are many carvings of ships, chariots, horses, and human figures. The most famous are "the Begby Man" and "The Dancer." The trail to the petroglyphs is well maintained and has explanation signs at each stop. There are also some burial mounds nearby but we could not clearly determine which were the graves versus just ground.

The Dancer at Gullskar Rock Carving Field in Norway

Afternoon: We spent our afternoon driving to Stockholm stopping at one of the Burger King locations along the highway for a quick lunch. The drive on the freeway to Stockholm is uneventful unless you drive into towns like Orebro. Once in Stockholm we missed our exit and had to go into one of the tunnels and then double back. But we made it to the hotel using GPS.

We arrived in Stockholm around 6 pm (or 18:00) and checked into our hotel where we stayed for three nights.

Hotel: Hotel Frantz is a small boutique hotel centrally located in Stockholm. From the hotel, we were able to walk everywhere. The hotel is stylish; however, I found our family room to be extremely cramped.

We did not have much space to hang our clothes and kept most of them in suitcases because of that. There is parking at the hotel, and they served the best breakfast buffet.
https://www.hotelfrantz.com/

Dinner: We had dinner at **Nour**, a Michelin star restaurant that is influenced by Scandinavia and Japan.
https://restaurantnour.se/
My husband and I strive to have at least one dinner at a Michelin star restaurant or equivalent on our trips and this was it. It was a wonderful experience that started out with about five or six small pre-dinner bites followed by the actual five-course dinner. The dishes were executed to the highest standards.

Day 6: Runestones and Meatballs

Morning/Early Afternoon: Spend half a day exploring the runestones outside of Stockholm. The area around Lake Vallentuna called Runriket has the largest concentration of preserved runestones in Sweden. It is only a 30-minute drive from Stockholm.

Runestones are ancient billboard signs with messages written in Runic letters. My impression after visiting multiple runestones in Runriket is that runestones in this area were raised in honor of a dead family member, usually male, and most have a cross on them to signify transition from paganism to Christianity.

Getting to Runriket: set your GPS or Apple/Google maps destination to Jarlabankes Bridge and follow directions. We did not have any trouble getting to this place. Despite lack of English resources on the Runriket website
https://www.runriket.se/ the information boards at the Jarlabankes Bridge and almost at each stop on the route were provided in Swedish and English.

Fallbro Runestone U 142 in Sweden

Start at Jarlabankes Bridge, which has two runestones. Don't miss the Taby Church, which was built at the end of the 13th century. In addition to a runestone, this church is famous for its murals painted by Albertus Pictor in the 15th century. The most famous painting is "Death Playing Chess," which inspired the movie "The Seventh Seal" directed by Ingmar Bergman. Continue around the lake to see more runestones and learn about Viking families that lived in this area.

Lunch: We skipped lunch and grabbed some snacks at a gas station on the way.

"Death Playing Chess" painting inside Taby Church

Late Afternoon: Return the rental car in Stockholm, and either walk or take a taxi to the hotel.

Dinner: Have dinner at **Meatballs for the People**. How can you not have Swedish meatballs while in Sweden? The restaurant serves meatballs from a variety of meats such as chicken, beef, pork and more exotic meats like bear, reindeer, and moose for an extra charge. Dishes are served with mashed potatoes, gravy, lingonberry sauce, and pickled cucumbers. My kids loved this place so much that we came here for dinner again the following night. http://meatball.se/

Day 7: Stockholm Sightseeing

Morning: Take a guided tour of **Stockholm City Hall** and go up the tower for a bird's eye view of the city. The City Hall is famous for two reasons. First, it is the place where the annual Nobel Prize Banquet is held. Second, its tower is one of the few places that offers panoramic views of central Stockholm. You have to buy two separate tickets: one for the guided tour of the City Hall and another to go up the tower. Note you can only go up the tower in the summer. For more information see City Hall's website https://stadshuset.stockholm/en/

City Hall on a left and Riddarhomen church on a right in Stockholm, Sweden

Lunch: Have lunch at the café in City Hall.

Afternoon: Spend the afternoon walking in the Old Town, stopping at one of these major tourist attractions:
- **The Riddarholmen Church** is a medieval abbey and a burial place for all of Swedish rulers except Queen Kristina.

https://www.kungligaslotten.se/english/royal-palaces-and-sites/the-riddarholmen-church.html

- **Marten Trotzigs Grand** is the narrowest street in Stockholm.

- **Gamla Stans Polkagriskokeri** is an old fashioned candy shop where you can get famous salmiak licorice sweets. https://gamlastanspolkagriskokeri.se/

- **Stortorget** is the main square in Old Town Stockholm that dates back to the 15th century. https://www.visitstockholm.com/o/stortorget/

- **Stockholm Cathedral** is the oldest church in Stockholm. It has the famous Saint George and the Dragon sculpture, and a silver and ebony altarpiece. https://www.svenskakyrkan.se/stockholmsdomkyrkoforsamling/visiting

- **The Royal Palace** is the official residence of Sweden's King and is open to the public. https://www.kungligaslotten.se/english/royal-palaces-and-sites/the-royal-palace.html

- **The Royal Armory** is a museum that showcases ceremonial equipment, weapons, and costumes from Sweden's royal history. My children enjoyed looking at all the armor and weapons. I found the royal carriages collection fascinating. This museum is separate from the Royal Palace and thus, you need a separate ticket. https://livrustkammaren.se/en/home/visit/

Colorful buildings in Stortorget in Stockholm, Sweden

Swedish Fika: Fika is the Swedish term for a coffee break. We had coffee and cardamom buns at the **Fabrique bakery**. https://fabrique.se/

Dinner: My children insisted on having meatballs for dinner again, so we went back to **Meatballs for the People**. If you are not in the mood for meatballs, have the shrimp toast. http://meatball.se/

Day 8: Half-day in Stockholm and Overnight Boat to Helsinki

Morning: Pack up your bags and leave them at the hotel's reception. Visit one of the sites that you were too tired to see the day before. We went to see the **Stockholm Cathedral**.

Stockholm Cathedral in the distance in Stockholm, Sweden

Other sightseeing ideas include the **Vasa Ship** museum https://www.vasamuseet.se/en and the **Skansen** open air museum https://skansen.se/en/

Lunch: We had the best meal on our trip at **Lisa Elmqvist**. This is the seafood restaurant and market. We ordered the shellfish platter, smoked eel, goat cheese salad, fish soup, and

smoked salmon. Everything tasted delicious.
https://www.lisaelmqvist.se/

Afternoon: Return to the hotel, collect your luggage, and take a taxi to the Värtahamnen boat terminal.

Overnight Boat from Stockholm to Helsinki: There are two companies that offer an overnight boat cruise between Stockholm and Helsinki: Viking and Tallink Silja. We chose the Tallink Silja because it is considered more of a family and less of a party boat. To book go to https://en.tallink.com/book-a-cruise

Don't be surprised to find that your overnight boat is an actual cruise ship. Two-night cruises from Helsinki to Stockholm and back are very popular among Finns. And yes, you will see strollers packed with cases of duty-free beer. The boat has restaurants, a kid play area, live performances, duty-free shopping and even a sauna. We had dinner at an Italian restaurant, walked around the shops and then retreated to our cabins for the night.

Day 9: Helsinki Sightseeing

Morning: Arrive in Helsinki around 10:30 am. Either walk or get a taxi to your hotel.

Hotel: Hotel F6 is a boutique hotel centrally located and is a short walk from the ferry terminal, Esplanade Park, and the Helsinki Cathedral. The room at Hotel F6 was the most spacious of all the hotels on our trip. https://hotelf6.fi/

Lunch: Have lunch at a **Café and Restaurant Kappeli**, which used to be a gathering place for artists and writers in the late 19th and early 20th century. There is a café with counter service where you can sit yourself on one side, and a restaurant with a full table service on the other. We had a goat cheese salad and

a reindeer main dish plus coffee and a dessert.
https://www.raflaamo.fi/en/restaurant/helsinki/kappeli

Helsinki Cathedral in Helsinki, Finland

Afternoon: Spend visiting some of the most known Helsinki tourist sights, the majority of which are the churches. All sights can be reached on foot.

- **The Market Square** is located next to the harbor where one can buy food, furs, knitted gloves and other souvenirs.
- **The Stone of the Empress** is an obelisk with a double-headed eagle on the top erected in honor of Empress Alexandra during her first visit to Helsinki. Finland was under Russian rule between 1809 to 1917.
- **Helsinki Cathedral** is a neoclassical Lutheran church designed by the architect Carl Ludvig Engel. It is located in Senate Square across from the Government Palace, which was also designed by Engel.
  https://helsingintuomiokirkko.fi/en/
- **Uspenski Cathedral** is a red brick Orthodox church.
  https://www.hos.fi/en/
- **The Kamppi Chapel** offers a quiet place for reflection and prayer in the middle of the city. It is very minimalist

in decoration and looks like a giant egg from the outside.
https://www.kampinkappeli.fi/index/visit_1.html

- **Temppeliaukio Church** (The Rock Church) is a Lutheran church built into the rock by the brothers Timo and Tuomo Suomalainen in 1969 and is one of the top tourist attractions in Helsinki.
https://www.temppeliaukionkirkko.fi/en/index.html

Dinner: Take a waterbus from the Market Square to **Lonna Island** and have dinner at a restaurant there. It is a farm-to-table type restaurant. In addition to the restaurant, you can also go to sauna there. To make reservations for dinner go to https://www.lonna.fi/en/services/restaurant/ and don't forget to book round-trip tickets for the waterbus at https://www.frs-finland.fi/suomenlinna-lonna/

Leaving Helsinki to Lonna Island on a waterbus

Day 10: Suomenlinna, Shopping and Sauna

Morning: Take the waterbus to **Suomenlinna**, a sea fortress that was built starting in 1748 and provided defense to Sweden, Russia, and Finland. It is designated as a UNESCO World Heritage site for its unique and well-preserved military architecture. It is a must-see attraction in Helsinki. Our kids enjoyed exploring the cannons, tunnels, and other military structures. https://www.suomenlinna.fi/en/

Cannon at Suomenlinna in Helsinki, Finland

Lunch: Have lunch at **Adlerfelt** restaurant in Suomenlinna.

Afternoon: Take a waterbus back to Helsinki and go shopping along the Pohjoisesplanadi across from the Esplanade Park. Suggested stores include:
1. **Marimekko** for clothes and home accessories
   https://www.marimekko.com/us_en/
2. **Iittala** for Finnish made glassware
   https://www.iittala.com/en-gb/about-us
3. **Akateeminen** for books
   https://www.akateeminen.com/en/

4. **Stockmann** for everything else you may need
    https://info.stockmann.com/info/stockmann-in-brief/

Dinner: We went back to the **Kapelli** restaurant for dinner. We were able to get seated right away without a reservation.

Evening: Sauna is an integral part of Finnish life. It is recommended to sit in a hot sauna for about 10 minutes, followed by a plunge into a lake or pool (cold shower can work as well), then rest to bring your body to its normal temperature, and repeat. Our hotel did not have a sauna so we went to the public one at **Allas Sea Pool**.
https://allasseapool.fi/?lang=en

Day 11: Day trip to Porvoo

Morning: Rent a car for 24 hours so that you can make a day trip outside of Helsinki but also have a car to get to the airport the next morning to catch your flight back home. We picked up a car at the Olympia terminal, a 15-20 minute walk from our hotel.

Main Square in Porvoo, Finland

Getting to Porvoo: Set your GPS or Apple/Google maps to Porvoo. The drive is about 45 minutes from Helsinki. Once there we parked our car near the old town and continued to the town center on foot.

Porvoo is the second oldest town in Finland and is famous for its red colored riverside cottages. It is a small town with a square, lots of souvenir shops and cozy cafes to have a sweet treat and a coffee.

For more information about Porvoo and what to do see
https://www.visitporvoo.fi/en/sights/old-porvoo/

Porvoo Cathedral in Porvoo, Finland

Lunch: We had the famous Runeberg cake, named after the Finnish poet, at **Café Fanny**.

Afternoon: Walk to the Porvoo Cathedral, visit one of the art galleries in the old town, walk along the river, and do some shopping. On the drive back to the hotel, stop at the **Sibelius Monument** in Helsinki, which honors the most famous Finnish composer and violinist Jean Sibelius.

Dinner: Have dinner at the restaurant **Pompier** that is a short walk from the hotel. https://pompier.fi/espa/

Day 12: Take a flight back home

Drive to Helsinki airport, return the rental car and take a flight back home.

Bibliography:

1. CIA World Factbook website https://www.cia.gov/the-world-factbook/
2. Forbes currency exchange website https://www.forbes.com/advisor/money-transfer/currency-converter/
3. Library of Congress Blogs. "Finland: 100 Years of Independence – Global Legal Collection Highlights" by Elin Hofverberg https://blogs.loc.gov/
4. World Heritage Convention UNESCO website https://whc.unesco.org/en/list/583/

39675460R00018